Good Night, Forest Friends

A Cozy Goodnight Book for Little Dreamers

Where stars twinkle softly,
the moon hums a lullaby,
and every tiny paw and feather
finds its favorite cozy place to sleep.

Bear stretches wide and gives a yawn,
his forest day is nearly gone.
The stars above begin to gleam,
as Bear sinks into a cozy dream.

Can you give a big sleepy yawn like Bear?

Fox wiggles once, then gives a sigh,
as fireflies go drifting by.
She curls her tail and shuts her eyes,
beneath the stars and sleepy skies.

Can you curl up like Fox getting ready for sleep?

Owl's eyelids flutter, slow and low,
as moonlight makes her feathers glow.
She tucks her wings without a peep,
and nods her head to fall asleep.

Can you blink slowly like Owl before bed?

Fawn nestles in a grassy bed,
moonlight shining on her head.
Spots so soft and breathing deep,
she's slipping into forest sleep.

Can you lie still like Fawn, ready for sleep?

Raccoon curls up without a sound,
wrapped in leaves upon the ground.
Her stripey tail keeps snuggles tight,
and dreams begin to drift through night.

Can you make your body small and cozy like Raccoon?

Hedgehog hides beneath a bloom,
a sleepy yawn in forest gloom.
She snuggles down without a peep,
and slowly tumbles into sleep.

Can you yawn just like Hedgehog?

Bunny lifts her paws up high,
then tucks them as the stars drift by.
She finds a hill to rest her head,
and settles down in her leafy bed.

Can you stretch your paws like Bunny?

Squirrel sways upon her tree,
blinking slowly, sleepily.
Wrapped in tail and branch so tight,
she says "good night" and turns off light.

Can you wrap your arms like a tail around yourself?

Chipmunk clutches one last treat,
then rests her head and tiny feet.
She dreams of snacks and leafy dens,
with forest creatures, all her friends.

What would you dream of if you were Chipmunk?

Moose finds a place so soft and wide,
and lays his sleepy horns aside.
He breathes in deep the forest air,
then dreams without a single care.

Can you breathe in deep like Moose?

Skunk peeks out to see the moon,
and gives a yawn—she'll be asleep soon.
She snuggles near a mossy log,
as dreams roll in just like the fog.

Can you peek like Skunk, then yawn big?

Bluebird tucks her head with care,
a nest of feathers, soft and fair.
She sways and sighs upon her tree,
a songbird sleeping peacefully.

Can you tuck in like Bluebird with your blanket?

Opossum stretches, big and wide,
then gives a yawn she cannot hide.
She finds her branch and takes a seat,
and lets her dreams be soft and sweet.

Can you yawn and stretch like Opossum?

Wolf pup yawns and blinks so slow,
then rests his head and lets it go.
He listens to the nighttime breeze,
and drifts to sleep beneath the trees.

Can you breathe softly like the wolf pup?

Can you spot the kitten licking an ice cream cone?

All the forest friends now rest,
in places that they love the best.
With dreams so warm, and hearts so light,
they drift into the softest night.

Can you find where each friend sleeps?

Now close your eyes and snuggle tight,
you've shared the forest's sleep tonight.
With every friend and dream in sight...
Good night, sweet one. Good night.

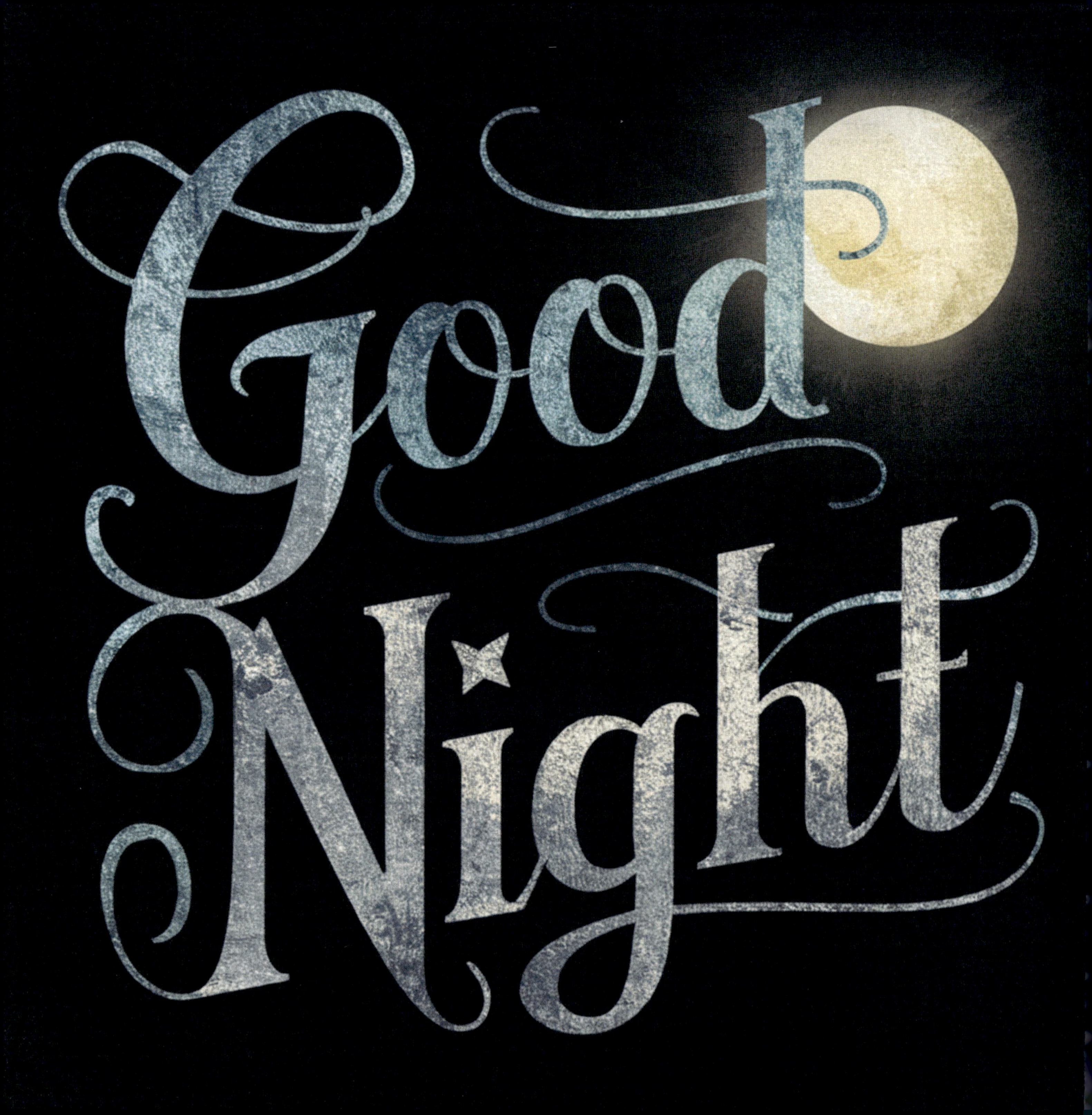
Good
Night